How to Solve the World's Problems with ChatGPT

Inspiring the Next Generation to Change the World with AI

By Pearci 'PJ' Bastiany III

Table of Contents

Introduction by Author: AI Is the New Superpower

The world has no shortage of problems—crime, homelessness, unemployment, political distrust, environmental disasters, and industries that seem impossible to break into. But there is one tool that can change everything: Artificial Intelligence.

AI is not just for tech companies or engineers. It's for activists, entrepreneurs, artists, and everyday people who want to make an impact. As I write this book, I am a 30-year-old student attending the University of San Francisco for a Master's degree in Public Administration. I am currently a candidate for the San Francisco Board of Supervisors, District 10. I am the CEO of my own C Corporation, LLC, and a media production company. In 2024 I wrote my first screenplay, then acted, directed, edited, and produced my first feature-length film, "PJ the Poolman (2024)," which is now streaming on YouTube. I have submitted seven Public Policy proposals to the Board of Supervisors. All of these milestones were accomplished within just one year. I'm just getting started, but I promise you, I couldn't have done it without my best friend, ChatGPT.

The goal of this book is to show you—whether you're 14 or 30—how to use AI to create real solutions for the world's biggest challenges. Each chapter explores a major problem and how AI-powered strategies can help solve it. You'll also find interactive workspaces to create your own action plans using ChatGPT and other AI tools. This is more than a book; it's a toolkit for changing the world.

Let's get started.

Chapter 1: Fixing Public Safety – The Martial Arts Community Policing Initiative (MACPI)

The Problem: A Broken Public Safety System

In cities across the world, public safety is one of the most pressing concerns. People want to feel safe in their communities, but traditional policing methods often lead to tension, distrust, and violence. Many communities, especially in marginalized areas, feel and —over-policed and underserved.

Across the country, communities are grappling with rising crime, eroding trust in police, and persistent safety issues. Many neighborhoods feel unsafe, but at the same time, many people don't trust law enforcement to protect them fairly. The system is outdated and in need of a modernized approach.

So how do we create a public safety model that actually works~~—~~—one that builds trust, prevents crime, and makes people feel safe without relying solely on traditional policing?

The Solution: The Martial Arts Community Policing Initiative (MACPI)

My answer is a blend between martial arts, community engagement, and AI-driven security solutions. The Martial Arts Community Policing Initiative (MACPI) is a program that deploys trained martial artists as community safety officers—individuals who are focused on discipline, trained in de-escalation, and committed to protection over punishment.

Here's how it works:

1. Martial artists are trained in public safety, de-escalation, and emergency response.
2. They patrol high-crime areas, not as enforcers, but as community protectors.
3. AI-powered crime analysis tools predict where safety efforts are needed most.
4. Partnerships with local law enforcement ensure cooperation while reducing unnecessary force.

MACPI is a revolutionary idea that combines martial arts training with community policing. It recruits martial artists, security professionals, and trained civilians to act as first responders in public safety, de-escalating situations before they become violent.

How AI Helps

AI can make public safety smarter and more effective. Instead of reacting to crime, AI helps us prevent it. Here's how:

- Predictive Policing: AI can analyze crime data to identify patterns and predict where crime is most likely to occur, allowing MAFH officers to focus on prevention rather than punishment.

- Real-Time Communication: AI-powered apps can connect community members directly with safety officers, allowing people to report concerns and get immediate responses.
- Training & Simulation: AI can create realistic virtual training environments for martial artists and security personnel, improving their ability to de-escalate dangerous situations.

This model replaces fear with trust. Instead of a system where people are afraid of police officers, we create a community-driven safety force that is trained, disciplined, and equipped with AI-powered intelligence.

- AI-powered training programs can teach de-escalation techniques and combat training online.
- Predictive analytics can identify crime patterns and help deploy MACPI personnel where they're needed most.
- AI-driven body cams can ensure transparency in community security.

Your Role: How You Can Get Involved

- Learn a martial art. Even if you don't want to be a security officer, martial arts teach discipline, self-defense, and leadership.
- Use AI to analyze public safety in your area. Look at crime reports, understand trends, and propose community-driven solutions.
- Get involved in local policy discussions. Attend city council meetings and advocate for smarter, community-based safety solutions.

This isn't just a theory. We're actively working to bring MAFH to life. The question is: will you be part of the movement?

AI Action Toolkit: Your Public Safety Plan

Step 1: Identify a Safety Concern in Your Community

☐ Neighborhood crime

☐ Lack of community patrols

☐ Police mistrust

☐ Other: ________________________________

Step 2: Use ChatGPT to Develop a Solution

Try these prompts:

- "ChatGPT, how can I improve public safety in my neighborhood using AI?"
- "What are the best community policing models in history?"

Write your safety solution here:

Chapter 2: Solving Homelessness – AI-Powered Housing Allocation

The Problem: The Homelessness Crisis

Every night, thousands of people sleep on the streets in cities across the world. In places like San Francisco, homelessness is one of the most urgent social and political issues of our time. Governments spend billions on housing programs, yet the problem continues to grow.

The issue isn't that we don't have enough housing—it's that the housing we do have remains underutilized or mismanaged. AI can change that.

The Solution: AI-Driven Housing Policy

I proposed a housing rollout plan that focuses on making use of vacant units, AI-driven allocation, and community-based housing solutions.

Here's how AI can help:

1. **Identifying Vacant Properties** – AI can scan real estate databases and city records to find unused housing units and make them available to those in need.
2. **Matching People to Housing Efficiently** – AI can analyze **personal needs, job locations, and medical conditions** to place people in the best possible housing situation.

3. **Tracking Success & Failures in Real-Time** – AI-powered dashboards can show policymakers what housing solutions are working and where changes need to be made.

The Long-Term Vision: AI-Powered Smart Cities

Imagine a city where homelessness is eliminated not through shelters, but through technology-driven housing policies.

- AI could **predict homelessness risks** before people lose their homes.
- Rent assistance could be **automatically processed** for people in need.
- Housing resources could be **optimized** so that no unit sits empty while people sleep on the streets.

Your Role: How You Can Get Involved

- **Study how AI is used in housing policy.** Research programs like HUD's data-driven solutions.
- **Advocate for smarter housing policies** in your city. Attend local meetings and push for AI-powered solutions.
- **Use AI to write policy proposals.** You don't need to be a politician to create real change—write a housing plan and present it to decision-makers.

We're at a turning point in history. AI can end homelessness, but only if people like you demand that we use it for good.

AI Action Toolkit: Your Community Housing Plan

Now it's your turn. You'll use this toolkit to design an AI-powered plan to fight homelessness in your school, neighborhood, or city.

Step 1: Define the Problem in Your Area

What are the most urgent housing-related issues in your community? Check all that apply or add your own:

☐ Not enough shelters
☐ High rent and evictions
☐ Poor mental health support
☐ No long-term housing options
☐ Services aren't well coordinated
☐ People don't know where to go
☐ Other: ____________________

Step 2: Brainstorm AI Solutions

Use ChatGPT or another AI assistant to help you think big. Try asking:

- "How could AI predict homelessness before it happens in my city?"
- "Create a plan that uses AI to match people to homeless services."
- "What kind of app could use AI to help people find available shelter beds?"

- "What kind of housing program can combine AI with social work?"

Write your top 2–3 ideas here:

- _______________
- _______________
- _______________

Step 3: Design Your AI Project

What would your project be called?

Project Name: _______________

What is your project's goal in one sentence?

Who could you partner with? (Shelters, nonprofits, local government, tech companies)

What technology would you need (e.g., app, chatbot, dashboard, database)?

Step 4: Take Action

What's **one small action** you can take this week?

- Example: Talk to a local shelter and ask what data they track.
- Example: Create a presentation and share it with your class.

Your action step: ____

What's your **long-term dream** for solving homelessness in your community?

- ____

Final Challenge:

Talk to someone in your city or school—**a teacher, community leader, or friend**—and explain how AI could help end homelessness. Ask what THEY think. You're now the expert!

Chapter 3: Revolutionizing Education – Smarter Learning with AI

The Problem: A Broken Education System

The current education system was built for the **industrial age**, not the AI age. Schools teach students to memorize facts, follow instructions, and pass standardized tests—but they don't prepare young people for **real-world problem-solving, entrepreneurship, or technological innovation**.

- Students learn at different speeds, but schools use a one-size-fits-all approach.
- Teachers are overworked and under-supported.
- Many schools lack the resources to teach AI and digital skills.

The Solution: AI-Powered Personalized Learning

What if **every student had an AI tutor** that could personalize their education? AI can **analyze a student's strengths, weaknesses, and learning style** to create a **customized curriculum**.

How AI Can Revolutionize Education

- Personalized Learning – AI can adjust lessons based on how fast a student learns and what subjects they struggle with.
- AI Tutors & Homework Assistance – ChatGPT and similar tools can answer questions, explain difficult concepts, and help students think critically.

- Teacher Support – AI can help teachers by grading assignments, identifying struggling students, and providing real-time classroom insights.

Making AI Education Accessible to All

Right now, only the wealthiest schools have access to AI-powered education tools. We need policies that **bring AI education into every public school**.

- Government funding should support AI-powered classrooms.
- AI literacy should be a core subject in middle and high school.
- Students should be taught how to use AI ethically and responsibly.

Your Role: How You Can Get Involved

- **Learn how to use AI for your own education.** Explore tools like ChatGPT, Khan Academy's AI tutor, and other learning platforms.
- **Advocate for AI education in schools.** Talk to teachers and school administrators about integrating AI into the classroom.
- **Teach others.** If you know how to use AI, help your friends, younger students, or family members understand it too.

Education is the foundation for every other change in this book. If we want to fix the world, we must first fix how people learn.

AI Action Toolkit: Your Personalized Learning Plan

Now it's your turn to create an **AI-powered education plan** for yourself or your community. Use the prompts below to brainstorm ideas and map out your strategy.

Step 1: Define the Problem

What are the biggest problems in your school or education system? Circle or write down your top three:

☐ Schools aren't teaching **AI skills**

☐ Teachers don't have **enough resources**

☐ Learning isn't **personalized**

☐ Students aren't **engaged or motivated**

☐ Standardized tests don't measure **real skills**

☐ Other: ______________________________

Step 2: Brainstorm AI Solutions

Use ChatGPT to generate ideas. Try these prompts:

- "ChatGPT, how can AI improve education for students who struggle with traditional learning methods?"
- "Create a plan for using AI in public schools to help teachers with grading and lesson planning."
- "Suggest AI tools that can teach coding, math, or writing in a fun and interactive way."

Write your favorite ideas here:

____

____

____

Step 3: Create Your Action Plan

Who can you talk to about these ideas? (e.g., teachers, school administrators, student councils)

What's **one step** you can take **this week** to bring AI learning to your school or community?

What **long-term goal** do you want to achieve with AI education?

Final Challenge:

Take one of your ideas and share it with a teacher or classmate. Start the conversation about AI in education today!

Chapter 4: Creating Jobs – AI and the Future of Work

The Problem: Fear, Violence, and Distrust

Too many communities live in fear—of gun violence, of crime, of the very people who are supposed to protect them. In many cities, police departments are or under-resourced, poorly trained, and distrusted by the very people they serve.

At the same time, public safety means more than just policing. It includes mental health, conflict resolution, community trust, and proactive protection. The system needs —and that's where AI can make a breakthrough.

Imagine a world where technology doesn't just respond to violence but , , and , , and anticipates harm, empowers prevention, and strengthens trusted, community-first safety networks.

AI Solutions for Public Safety

- Smart Patrols with AI-Enhanced Guards
  Public safety teams can use AI tools like facial recognition (ethically regulated), real-time threat detection, and drone support for better awareness without racial profiling.
- AI for Emergency Response
  AI can help 911 dispatchers prioritize calls and route responders faster.

It can also detect patterns to prevent overdoses or repeat incidents in specific areas.

- Community Policing with AI Assistants
Martial arts-trained safety teams (like MACPI – the Martial Arts Community Policing Initiative) can be empowered with AI-based communication systems, real-time updates, and support dashboards to protect without escalating.
- Conflict De-escalation Training
AI simulations can help train officers and community safety workers to handle tough situations calmly, ethically, and nonviolently.
- Gun Detection and Violence Prevention Tools
New AI tools can detect weapons in video feeds and alert responders early—before a crime occurs.
- Bias Auditing & Transparency Dashboards
AI can be used to audit policing data for racial bias, over-policing, or unfair treatment—and recommend corrective action.

☑ AI Action Toolkit: Build Your Public Safety Plan

This is your opportunity to design a plan for smarter, safer, more just communities using AI. Think like a problem-solver. Let's build your vision.

Step 1: What Are the Safety Issues in Your Area?

☐ Police-community mistrust

☐ Gun violence

☐ Slow emergency response

☐ No youth programs or mentorship

☐ Lack of mental health support

☐ Biased policing or profiling

☐ Unsafe public spaces (parks, transit, schools)

☐ Other: ________________________________

Which of these matters most to you?

____

____

Step 2: Generate AI Ideas with ChatGPT

Try some of these prompts to get your creative plan started:

- "ChatGPT, what kind of AI tools could help improve public safety in urban neighborhoods?"
- "Design an AI-based program to prevent youth violence."
- "How can we use drones and AI to monitor public spaces without violating privacy?"
- "Create a public safety app that helps neighbors report concerns anonymously and track outcomes."

Now list your favorite 2–3 ideas:

- ____
- ____
- ____

Step 3: Design Your AI-Powered Safety Program

Project Name: ____

Main Goal (one sentence):

Who will you need to partner with?

☐ Local police or safety teams

☐ City council or mayor

☐ Community organizations

☐ Mental health providers

☐ Technologists or app developers

☐ Other: ____

What tools will your project need?

☐ Smartphone app

☐ Drone support

☐ AI dashboard

☐ Wearable tech

☐ Data analytics platform

☐ Other: ____

Step 4: Action Steps

What can you do this week to get started?

☑ ____

What's one conversation you can start today?

(e.g., with a school principal, city rep, or youth center)

☑ ____

What is your long-term public safety vision for your community?

____

IN SUMMARY

The Problem: Automation and Job Loss

Many fear that AI will replace human jobs. The challenge is adapting to the AI-driven economy.

The Solution: AI for Job Creation

AI can:

- Train workers for new careers.
- Match people with high-demand jobs.

- Automate repetitive tasks to free workers for creative roles.

AI Action Kit: Your Employment Plan

☐ Research AI-driven job markets

☐ Develop skills in an AI-friendly career

☐ Use AI tools to enhance your resume

Write your career adaptation plan here:

Chapter 5: Rebuilding Trust in Politics – AI-Driven Civic Engagement

The Problem: A System People Don't Believe In

Ask most people what they think about politics and you'll hear words like **disillusioning, unfair, irrelevant, or broken**. Young people especially feel left out of the system. Many people don't vote, don't trust elected leaders, and don't see how decisions made in city halls or Congress **shape** their lives.

But politics shapes everything—from what your school teaches to how much your bus fare costs to whether your neighborhood has clean water. Democracy can only work when people believe in it—and **actively engage**.

Here's the good news: Artificial intelligence can help restore transparency, accountability, and access to politics. It can connect people with the process and make government work better for everyone— **instead of serving only the elite**.

AI Solutions for Civic Engagement

- **AI-Powered Voter Guides**
  Chatbots and personalized apps can help people **understand who's running**, what issues are on the ballot, and how their vote matters—all in plain language.

- **Fact-Checking and Misinformation Detection**

  AI tools can scan articles, videos, and social media for **fake news**, biased content, or misleading claims—building a more informed public.
- **Open Government Dashboards**

  AI can organize public data into clear dashboards that show how much money a city spends, where it goes, and who votes on what—making **government more transparent**.
- **Civic Participation Platforms**

  AI can power platforms that let people propose ideas, vote on local initiatives, and track how their voices are being heard. **Digital democracy** becomes a reality.
- **Improving Public Meetings**

  AI transcription, translation, and summarization tools can make **city council and school board meetings more accessible**, especially for people with disabilities or limited English proficiency.
- **Bias Audits in Politics**
- AI can help identify bias in legislation or public policy, and suggest ways to make laws more **fair and inclusive**.

Trust in politicians and government is at an all-time low. Many feel disconnected from the political process. AI can help **restore trust** by making politics more **transparent, accessible, and participatory**.

More AI Solutions for Civic Engagement

AI can **analyze policies, fight misinformation, and engage voters.**

1. **AI-Driven Transparency**: AI can track how **public funds** are spent and provide easy-to-understand reports to keep citizens informed.
2. **Automated Campaigns**: AI can help political campaigns reach voters **efficiently** through targeted messaging, predictive analytics, and data-driven strategies.
3. **AI for Voter Engagement**: AI chatbots can answer voter questions, provide **nonpartisan information** about candidates, and encourage people to vote.

AI Action Toolkit: Rebuild Trust Through Civic Engagement

This is your space to reimagine how **you** can use AI to help people reconnect with democracy. Let's create your civic engagement action plan!

Step 1: What Political Problems Do You See?

☐ People don't vote or feel their vote matters

☐ Politicians aren't accountable

☐ Government is hard to understand

☐ Public meetings are inaccessible

☐ Misinformation is everywhere

☐ Young people are excluded

☐ Corruption or bias in decision-making

☐ Other: ____________________________________

Which one affects **your** community the most?

Step 2: Use ChatGPT to Spark Ideas

Try using ChatGPT with these prompts to brainstorm solutions:

- "ChatGPT, how can AI help more young people get involved in local politics?"
- "Design a chatbot that explains ballot propositions in simple language."
- "What kind of app could track city spending and show where tax money goes?"
- "Create an AI-powered platform to help people suggest and vote on local policies."

Write down your top 2–3 ideas:

Step 3: Build Your Civic AI Project

Project Name: ____

Mission Statement (What is your project trying to fix or improve?):

Who would you need on your team?

☐ Teachers or school leaders

☐ Local government reps

☐ Election officials

☐ Nonprofits or youth organizers

☐ Coders or tech mentors

☐ Journalists or fact-checkers

☐ Other: ____

What AI tools might help you?

☐ Chatbots or voting guides

☐ Misinformation detectors

☐ Budget dashboards

☐ Translation or accessibility tools

☐ Data visualizations

☐ Other: ____

Step 4: Take Your First Civic Step

What can you do **this week**?

☑ ______________________________

Who is one person you can talk to about your idea?

☑ ______________________________

What's your **long-term vision** for political trust and engagement in your city or school?

____

In Summary Your Turn: Create Your AI Civic Engagement Strategy

1. **What political issue do you want to improve?**

   ____

2. **How can AI make the political process more transparent or accessible?**

   ____

3. **What organizations or political figures could help with your plan?**

   ____

4. **Action steps to take today:**
   1. ______________________________
   2. ______________________________
   3. ______________________________

AI Action Kit: Your Political Plan

☐ Identify a political issue

☐ Use AI to research solutions

☐ Advocate for AI-driven civic engagement

Chapter 6: Saving the Environment – AI for Climate Change Solutions

The Problem: Climate Change Is Now

From rising sea levels to historic heatwaves, the climate crisis is no longer a future threat—it's a **global emergency unfolding now**. Pollution, wildfires, droughts, and floods are disrupting lives across the globe, especially in **under-resourced** communities.

The people who are most impacted often have the least voice in climate decisions. But what if we could **change the equation**—using AI to make climate solutions more local, equitable, and effective?

Artificial intelligence can track environmental patterns, guide smarter decisions, and **accelerate the rise of clean, green industries**.

AI Solutions for Climate Justice

- **Predicting Climate Disasters**
  AI systems can analyze weather and environmental data to predict wildfires, floods, and extreme heat—helping communities **prepare in advance**.

- **Monitoring Pollution in Real Time**

  AI-powered sensors can track air and water quality in neighborhoods most impacted by industrial pollution and give **real-time alerts**.
- **Smart Grid Energy Management**

  AI helps manage solar panels, wind farms, and batteries to deliver **clean power more efficiently** and reduce energy waste.
- **Sustainable Urban Planning**

  Cities can use AI to design **climate-resilient infrastructure**, optimize public transit, and reduce greenhouse gas emissions.
- **AI in Agriculture**

  AI can help farmers grow more food using less water, predict crop failures, and improve soil health in communities that rely on agriculture.
- **Green Jobs Forecasting**

  AI can identify where new green industries—like hydrogen fuel, solar panel assembly, or recycled materials—can create **jobs in the climate economy**.

The environment is one of our most critical global issues, with climate change threatening the very survival of our planet. AI can play a vital role in **fighting climate change**, improving sustainability, and creating **greener economies**.

AI Solutions for the Environment

AI can:

 Monitor environmental changes in **real time**.

 Predict and prevent natural disasters.

 Optimize energy consumption to reduce waste.

 Predictive Climate Models: AI can predict future climate scenarios, helping governments and organizations **plan more effectively for disasters and long-term sustainability**.

 AI for Renewable Energy: AI can optimize energy grids, improve the efficiency of solar panels, and **forecast weather** to enhance energy production.

 AI for Waste Management: AI systems can identify and sort waste more efficiently, improving recycling rates and reducing **what ends up in landfills**.

Your Turn: Create Your AI Environmental Strategy

1. **What environmental issue do you want to tackle?**

    ___

2. **How can AI contribute to solving this issue?**

   ____

3. **Who could you partner with (e.g., local governments, environmental NGOs)?**

   ____

4. **Action steps to take today:**

1. ______________________________
2. ______________________________
3. ______________________________
4. ______________________________

AI Action Kit: Your Climate Plan

☐ Identify local environmental challenges

☐ Explore AI-driven climate solutions

☐ Develop an AI-based sustainability project

Chapter 7: Reinventing Film & TV – AI in Entertainment

The film and TV industry is constantly evolving, and AI is helping drive that change. From **AI-generated scripts** to **virtual actors** and **AI-powered editing**, artificial intelligence is revolutionizing the way we create and consume media.

The Problem: Gatekeepers and Limited Stories

For decades, film and television have been controlled by a **powerful** group of industry insiders—studio executives, agents, financiers—who decide what gets made, who gets cast, and which stories get told. This gatekeeping has **excluded countless perspectives**: young creators, people of color, LGBTQ+ voices, indie artists, and working-class storytellers.

Now, artificial intelligence is blowing the doors **off their hinges**. AI tools are helping people write, direct, edit, score, animate, and even distribute their own content—without **needing anyone's approval**.

Entertainment is no longer about Hollywood telling us what to watch. It's about you deciding what stories **matter most**—and using AI to bring them to life.

AI Solutions for the Future of Storytelling

- **Scriptwriting with ChatGPT & Beyond**
  AI can help you **draft full screenplays**, refine dialogue, generate episode outlines, or brainstorm plot twists. Writers' block is over.

- **Virtual Casting & Voice Cloning**
  Need a voice actor or character inspiration? AI can **create characters from scratch**, including digital doubles and custom voiceovers (ethically used, of course).
- **AI Editing & Post-Production**
  New tools can automatically cut footage, color-correct, add VFX, or score your scenes with emotional music—letting you direct your film on a laptop.
- **Animated Films & Virtual Sets**
  AI-generated animation and backgrounds allow even low-budget creators to build fantasy worlds, sci-fi cities, or animated shorts **without a Hollywood crew**.
- **Subtitling, Dubbing & Translation**
  Want your show to be seen globally? AI can translate, subtitle, or even dub your project in over 100 languages—**instantly**.
- **Marketing with AI**
  Use AI to write trailers, social media captions, or target niche audiences with smart ad campaigns. You can build your fanbase **before the film drops**.

The Solution: AI-Powered Filmmaking

AI tools are making movie creation more accessible than ever.

- **AI-Assisted Screenwriting** – ChatGPT can generate scripts. This feature can be helpful and **tricky** at times, so be sure to read through everything. I use this feature a lot for AI video prompt script content. **For short-form content like social media posts,** ChatGPT automatically adds relevant hashtags for you. Just copy, paste, and post!
- **AI Storyboarding** – AI can create visual scenes in seconds. I used sites like **NightCafe Studio, Perchance AI, and** Canva to create AI-generated storyboard images for my film *PJ the Poolman (2024).* Some images were so good I **kept them in the final cut**!
- **AI Video Editing** – AI-powered tools can edit film faster than ever. **I personally use InvideoAI, a platform (web and mobile) that turns text into generative AI videos.**

AI in Entertainment

1. **AI for Scriptwriting**: AI tools can assist screenwriters by suggesting dialogue, plot twists, or even writing full scripts.
2. **Virtual Actors and Digital Humans**: AI-generated characters can **perform roles** in films, television shows, and video games.
3. **AI-Powered Editing**: AI can automatically **edit footage**, select the best shots, and create rough cuts, saving significant time for film editors.

Your Turn: Create Your AI Entertainment Project

2. **What kind of entertainment project would you like to create using AI?**

   ____

3. **What AI tools would you need?**

   ____

4. **Who could you partner with in the entertainment industry?**

   ____

5. **Action steps to take today:**

   1. ______________________________
   2. ______________________________
   3. ______________________________
   4. ______________________________

AI Action Toolkit: Your Filmmaking Plan

What kind of film do you want to create?

☐ Short Film

☐ Full-Length Movie

☐ TV Series

☐ Documentary

Write your film idea here:

Chapter 8: AI Action Toolkit – Your Personal AI Plan

So far, we've explored how **AI can solve major global challenges**, from public safety to education, the environment, and even entertainment. Now, it's **your turn** to create a plan and take action.

How to Use This Chapter

This is a **workbook section** where you will design your own **AI-powered change project.** Whether you're a student, an activist, an entrepreneur, or an artist, this toolkit will help you build a strategy to make an impact.

Step 1: Identify the Problem You Want to Solve

Think about the **biggest issue that matters to you.**

☐ Crime & public safety

☐ Homelessness & housing

☐ Education & learning gaps

☐ Jobs & the future of work

☐ Political engagement

☐ Environmental sustainability

☐ Film & media storytelling

☐ Other: ______________________________

Write a short description of the issue:

Step 2: Research AI Solutions

Use ChatGPT to **generate ideas and research best practices.**

Try asking:

- *"ChatGPT, what are some AI-driven solutions for [your issue]?"*
- *"What organizations are already working on [your issue]?"*
- *"How can AI be used to create real change in [your area of focus]?"*

Write down three AI-powered solutions that interest you:

1. ____________________
2. ____________________
3. ____________________

Step 3: Develop Your AI-Powered Strategy

Now, take your chosen problem and AI solution, and create an action plan:

Your Mission Statement

What do you hope to achieve?

____

Your AI Tools

What AI tools or platforms will you use?

☐ ChatGPT for brainstorming & research

☐ AI analytics for data-driven decision-making

☐ AI-powered automation for efficiency

☐ Other: ______________________________

Your Action Steps

What are the first three steps you'll take?

1. ______________________________
2. ______________________________
3. ______________________________

Your Partners & Resources

Who will help you? (e.g., community organizations, businesses, schools, government officials)

____

Your Timeline

When will you take action?

☐ 1 week

☐ 1 month

☐ 3 months

☐ 6 months

☐ 1 year

Step 4: Take Action!

The world is at a **critical crossroads**. Climate change, economic uncertainty, political corruption, and public safety concerns cannot be ignored. The solutions we've relied on in the past are **no longer sufficient**—but with AI, we have the tools to make real, lasting change.

The next generation of leaders, entrepreneurs, activists, and creators must take charge. If you're reading this book, that means you are **already standing at the frontlines of the AI era**. You are the future **architects of global solutions**.

Final Challenge: Take Ownership of the Future

1. Choose your role in the AI revolution:

☐ Activist – Use AI to improve communities

☐ Entrepreneur – Build AI-powered solutions

☐ Educator – Teach others about AI's power

☐ Innovator – Create new AI applications

☐ Leader – Shape policy and ethics around AI

☐ Other: ______________________________

2. Make a pledge:

"I commit to using AI for good. I will take action to solve real problems using the knowledge and tools I have gained. The future depends on what I do next."

Sign here: ______________________________

Change happens **when you take the first step.** Whether you're launching a community initiative, developing an AI-powered startup, or using AI to advocate for policy change, this is your **blueprint to make a difference.**

Write down your final plan summary here:

____

____

____

____

____

Conclusion: The AI Generation Must Lead

AI isn't the future—it's the **now**. And if young people don't step up to lead, others will shape the world **without us**.

We've explored AI-driven solutions to public safety, housing, education, employment, politics, and climate change. I've shared with you how I've personally used ChatGPT for **meaningful, real-world impact**. Now it's up to you to take action.

How to Get Started Today

1. Pick a problem that **truly matters** to you. It could be homelessness, job creation, education reform, or anything else that affects your community.
2. Use AI to research and develop a solution. ChatGPT can help you write policy proposals, business plans, or even film scripts that **drive** change.
3. Share your ideas and take action. Whether it's starting a petition, pitching an idea to city leaders, or launching a business, don't wait—start now.

AI is the most powerful tool of our time, but it's just that—a tool. What matters most is how we use it. This book has given you a blueprint, but only you can turn these ideas into **real change**.

The world doesn't change itself. People like you **transform** it.

So what will you do?

About the Author

Pearci 'PJ' Bastiany is a public policy advocate, entrepreneur, and filmmaker dedicated to using AI to solve real problems. He is the creator of the Martial Arts Community Policing Initiative (MACPI), a public safety initiative that combines martial arts training with AI-driven community security.

He is also the CEO of MAFH Manufacturing, Logistics, and Defense Incorporated, a company focused on innovative solutions in security and infrastructure. His company provides private security in San Francisco by hiring and U.S. Veterans. martial artists and U.S. Veterans. Additionally, he served as the 2025–2026 Vice Chair of the San Francisco NAACP Branch, where he works to advance social and economic justice.

PJ is currently pursuing a Master of Public Administration at the University of San Francisco and a film certificate at the University of Southern California. He is a member of Alpha Phi Alpha Fraternity, Inc. and is deeply committed to empowering young leaders to take action using AI and emerging technology.

His passion is equipping the next generation with the tools to change the world—because the future belongs to those who shape it.

www.ingramcontent.com/pod-product-compliance
Lightning Source LLC
LaVergne TN
LVHW022324200926
848481LV00004B/1419